The Balanced Journey

Harnessing Ancient Wisdom and Modern Planning for Aligned Intentions and Spiritual Growth

ELIZABETH GODDARD

The Balanced Journey
Harnessing Ancient Wisdom and Modern Planning for Aligned Intentions and Spiritual Growth

ELIZABETH GODDARD

The Balanced Journey

Harnessing Ancient Wisdom and Modern Planning for Aligned Intentions and Spiritual Growth

This edition is published by Revive Your Soul Publishing in 2024 © Copyright 2024 Elizabeth Goddard All rights reserved.

No part of this publication may be reproduced, stored in a retrieval system, or transmitted in any form or by any means without permission of the publisher.

ISBN: 978-1-9163577-5-4

I dedicate this book to
our ancestors who want to
share their wisdom now and to Serapis Bey for the
push I needed to get this out in the world

I dedicate this book to
our ancestors who want to
share their wisdom now and to Serapis Bey for the
push I needed to get this out in the world

The Balanced Journey

WELCOME

My name is Elizabeth, and I am so glad you have decided to join me on this part of your journey.

When my life was in chaos, I turned to ancient practices and modernised them to help me reclaim some of the power I had lost.

They helped me gain clarity.

You will begin to inner-stand your purpose using your inner knowing. Our life purpose is everything. It is the beginning, the middle and the end.

Without purpose, we can get lost. And without purpose, we can live another person's life unintentionally.

Using your intuition, you can discover through these pages what you want and how to lean into creating a life that harnesses that.

Sending you loads of love

Elizabeth x

WELCOME

My name is Elizabeth, and I am so glad you have decided to join me on this part of your journey.

When my life was in chaos, I turned to ancient practices and modernised them to help me reclaim some of the power I had lost.

They helped me gain clarity.

You will begin to inner-stand your purpose using your inner knowing. Our life purpose is everything. It is the beginning, the middle and the end.

Without purpose, we can get lost. And without purpose, we can live another person's life unintentionally.

Using your intuition, you can discover through these pages what you want and how to lean into creating a life that harnesses that.

Sending you loads of love

Elizabeth x

> There is no greater agony than bearing an untold story inside you.
>
> Maya Angelou

CONTENTS

HOW TO USE — 15

HABIT OR RITUAL? — 19

CREATING YOUR MASTER LIST — 20

CREATING YOUR GOALS — 21

MASTER PLAN — 26

INDEX PAGE — 30

FUTURE LOG — 34

MONTHLY JOURNALING — 44

QUOTE REFERENCES — 350

How to Use

Welcome to Your Sacred Space.

This diary is a space for reflection, growth, and staying focused on what matters.

I created it when I struggled to find clarity and direction, and it has since become a valuable tool in helping me regain control of my life. What helped me the most was planning my days and breaking things down into manageable tasks. Ticking off each task as I completed it gave me a sense of accomplishment and kept me moving forward.

This diary is here to help you do the same. Whether you're setting goals, organising your thoughts, or checking off daily tasks, it's designed to help you stay on track and keep your focus where it needs to be.

How to use this diary

Master Plan
This is where you create the life you were born to live.
The Master Plan outlines your long-term goals, whether you are planning your holidays, a new home or car or creating a life you won't need a holiday from.

You can revisit it regularly to ensure you're still in alignment and keep returning to add or tweak as things change.

To help get your ideas flowing, use the 'Life I Don't Need a Holiday From' sheet, which breaks your life into different areas for easier brainstorming.

Once completed, you can transfer your ideas to the Master Plan.

Index Page

The Index Page is a practical tool for quickly locating information in your diary. Use it to keep track of anything important you might want to find later. For example, you might jot down something inspirational or a recipe for an immune booster. Write and record the page number in the index, briefly referencing the information.

Future Log

The Future Log will help you plan and organise events, tasks, and important dates, such as birthdays, anniversaries, and significant events.

Goals

Inspired by the Bagua map, instead of using it in a physical area, it allows you to be creative and to focus on what's important in different areas of your life, whether it's family, health, or career.
Use this space, along with your Master Plan, to stay clear on what you're manifesting, making sure your focus stays right where it needs to be.

Align & Begin

Start each month with three key questions: How do I feel? What do I want to achieve? What do I want to clear?
Journalling these questions will help you start the month with clarity and help you focus on what you do want. They will allow you to identify emotional blocks or distractions and focus on what you need to move forward.

Journal Prompts

Journaling is a powerful way to organise your thoughts and emotions. In the Journal Prompts section, jot down any thoughts or memories that arise throughout the month. These can be revisited for self-reflection, allowing you the flexibility to explore them when you are ready. Techniques like stream-of-consciousness writing can clear mental fog, and Reflective Journaling offers insights. Use this space to capture and return to your reflections as needed.

Rituals and Habits

Think about any rituals or habits you can incorporate into your day or week. These can help you stay aligned with your goals, overall health and well-being. If something doesn't fit, adjust it to work with your life.

Task List

The Task List does what it says; it lists your tasks. You can organise and track your tasks, making it easier to focus on what's most important and ensure nothing gets overlooked.

Month-to-View

The Month-to-View layout lets you plan and track your monthly tasks, appointments, and goals. Next to each number, there's a blank circle where you can mark the day of the week. This flexible format lets you customise the month and keep an overview of key dates.

Week-to-View

Map out your week in more detail in this section with your daily appointments, tasks, or events, helping you stay organised day by day.

Notes/Ideas

The Notes and Ideas pages are for generating ideas, capturing fleeting thoughts, or jotting down anything important that comes to mind. Use this section to write freely.

Reflection Page

The Reflection Page is a space to review your month. Consider what worked well and what didn't, how your goals or habits supported you, and what you've learned. Reflect on any patterns, challenges, or insights during the month. This section helps you pause, process your experiences, and refine your approach for the next month.

Feel free to use this diary however it best serves you. It's a flexible tool, so trust your instincts—if something doesn't feel right, change it. The most important thing is that it supports your growth in a way that works for you.

Vision Board Bingo

Creatively turn your goals into reality with Vision Board Bingo. Use the 12 boxes to list your goals—whether they're big aspirations, small wins, or habits and rituals you'd like to build. For example, you might include meditating daily, completing a project at work, or planning a weekend getaway.

As you reach each goal, cross it off—just like a bingo card! While creating your board, think about how you'll celebrate your wins. What will you do when you complete a line? How will you reward yourself for achieving a full house? Perhaps committing to a special treat or experience will keep you motivated.

Habit or Ritual?

The difference between a habit and a ritual is that a ritual has attitude!
Routines are actions that need to be done, like making your bed or taking a shower, whereas rituals are more meaningful practices.
Rituals do not have to be spiritual or religious.
Habits are beneficial. They help you through the gloop and when you are processing what has happened. They keep your focus and help you stay grounded firmly in your body and out of your head, which is crucial in keeping you out of rumination.

You may have a habit of making a cup of tea or coffee in the morning, but it might be at different times every day. You might make it while doing other things. However, a ritual would be more mindful. Each movement has meaning. For example, you might use a special cup and place it in a certain way. It might be the way you prepare a meal and set your table or how you prepare for your day.
Creating a routine will help your mind and body, and creating a safe space tells your body it is okay to relax and rest for a while. Living life with attitude.

Creating your Master List

The Bagua for Creating Your Master List

The Bagua Map is an ancient Feng Shui tool that maps out a space's energy flow (chi). It consists of nine sections, each representing a different aspect of life. Traditionally, it was used to balance and harmonise a home or environment. I have adapted it as a goal-setting and manifestation tool.

How the Bagua Works:

Each section of the Bagua corresponds to a specific life area. Traditionally, you would overlay the Bagua on your home's floor plan and evaluate and improve energy flow in these areas.

Converting the Bagua into a Goal-Setting Tool

In this adaptation, the Bagua becomes a blueprint for setting goals in key life areas. Instead of focusing on physical space, you'll use the Bagua to define and manifest personal goals, aligning actions and intentions with each life aspect.

Creating Your Goals

How to Use It for Goal-Setting

Use the Bagua sections to categorise your life goals. Incorporate affirmations, visualisations, and gratitude for each life area.

This approach transforms the Bagua into a holistic tool for personal growth, helping you balance all areas of life while achieving your goals.

When reviewing each section, consider the questions in each area to help you become more focused on your goals.

Wealth & Abundance	Fame & Reputation	Relationships & Love
• What does prosperity mean, and where do I want to create it? • How can I align my skills to attract increased income? • What steps can I take to invite abundance and receive it? • What strengths can I focus on to bring more prosperity and success to my business or life? • What causes do I care about that I can contribute to in time or money?	• What steps can I take to pursue a desired passion or goal? • How can I bring focus and courage to start on this dream, knowing it will enhance my sense of purpose? • How can I build trust, dependability, and positive influence in my relationships? • How can I handle challenges gracefully to preserve my character and respect from others?	• What qualities am I looking for in a partner, and how can I embody those qualities myself? • How can I build trust in myself and my partner to make a fearless commitment? • What relationships are meaningful to me? • How can I nurture relationships based on acceptance, empathy, and understanding?
Health	**Creativity & Children**	**Knowledge & Wisdom**
• How can I nurture my body with nourishing food, regular movement, and restful sleep to feel my best? • How can I prioritise my time and energy to maintain a healthy balance in all areas? • What fitness or movement routines can I enjoy that increase my strength and vitality? • What do I want to look like? • What self-care rituals can I embrace to honour my health and prevent burnout?	• What changes can I make to nurture this new chapter in life? • What can I do to bring deeper satisfaction and personal growth? • How can I create space in my day to allow inspiration and creativity to flow naturally? • How can I bring curiosity and joy into my life and nurture my inner child? • What can I do to bring positivity into each day?	• What are my values and goals? • How can I approach decisions confidently and align with my values and goals? • How can I align my actions and intentions to attract the correct situations? • How can I trust my inner voice and use my life experiences to guide me toward better choices? • Do I want to expand my knowledge, and where?
Career & Life Path	**Helpful People & Travel**	**Family & Ancestors**
• What type of work would align with my values and purpose? • What steps can I take to launch or expand a business that aligns with my strengths and passions? • How can I listen to my inner guidance and clarify my life's purpose? • What habit or ritual can I use to align with my purpose?	• How can I set boundaries and communicate my needs to ensure fair and respectful treatment? • How can I create strong connections with people who share mutual goals and values? • How can I reach out to others for assistance, creating a balanced and efficient workflow? • How can I attract supportive, trustworthy people into my life and work?	• What actions or habits can I adopt to create greater stability and security in my life? • How can I strengthen my foundations (emotional, financial, or relational) to feel more prepared and less stressed in difficult times? • How can I show understanding and compassion to improve family bonds and create a peaceful home environment?

Life is really simple, but we insist on making it complicated.

Confucius

The life I don't need a holiday from. The Nine Life Areas (and their Goal-Setting Focus)

Wealth & Abundance: Focuses on prosperity, financial well being, and material abundance.	**Fame & Reputation:** Represents your public image, recognition, and how others see you.	**Relationships & Love** Governs romantic and personal relationships.
Health: Focusing on your health and balance, as well as your physical, emotional, and mental health in all areas of life.	**Knowledge & Wisdom:** This area focuses on learning, personal development, and self-cultivation.	**Career & Life Path:** This area relates to your career, life's journey, and purpose.
Helpful People & Travel: This sector governs the presence of mentors, helpful people, and travel opportunities.	**Children & Creativity:** Connected to creativity, joy, and future projects, including children.	**Family & Ancestors:** Strengthening and bringing harmony in relationships with family.

Master Plan

How to Use This Section

This is where you design the life you were born to live. The Master Plan outlines your long-term goals, whether planning holidays, a new home or car or creating a life you won't need a holiday from. You can revisit it regularly to ensure you're still in alignment and keep returning to add or tweak as things change. To help get your ideas flowing, use the 'Life I Don't Need a Holiday From' sheet, which breaks your life into different areas for easier brainstorming. Once completed, you can transfer your ideas to this Master Plan.

-
-
-
-
-
-
-
-
-
-

Index Page

How to Use This Section

The Index Page is a practical tool for quickly locating information in your diary. Use it to keep track of anything important you might want to find later. For example, you might jot down something inspirational or a recipe for an immune booster.

Write and record the page number in the index, briefly referencing the information.

Future Log

Future Log

Vision Board Bingo

> "I remember the pain of being let down, of not having anyone there to support me, it was a big dark black hole, a place of nothingness, I was hiding in this cave of despair and not wanting to do what I was going to do.

Elizabeth Goddard · Finding Lily

Monthly Goals

Wealth & Abundance: Focuses on prosperity, financial well being, and material abundance.	**Fame & Reputation:** Represents your public image, recognition, and how others see you.	**Relationships & Love** Governs romantic and personal relationships.
Health: Focusing on your health and balance, as well as your physical, emotional, and mental health in all areas of life.	**Knowledge & Wisdom:** This area focuses on learning, personal development, and self-cultivation.	**Career & Life Path:** This area relates to your career, life's journey, and purpose.
Helpful People & Travel: This sector governs the presence of mentors, helpful people, and travel opportunities.	**Children & Creativity:** Connected to creativity, joy, and future projects, including children.	**Family & Ancestors:** Strengthening and bringing harmony in relationships with family.

Align & Begin

Journal all or some of these questions

How do I feel? What do I want to achieve? What do I want to clear?

Journal Prompts

For more clarity, use the space below to record anything that came up while journaling. Bullet below, and use the memory, question, thought, or emotion as a journal prompt when you feel ready.

-
-
-
-
-
-
-
-
-
-
-
-

Month to View

1.
2.
3.
4.
5.
6.
7.
8.
9.
10.
11.
12.
13.
14.
15.
16.
17.
18.
19.
20.
21.
22.
23.
24.
25.
26.
27.
28.
29.
30.
31.

Tasks

Weekly

Monday

Tuesday

Wednesday

Thursday

Friday

Saturday

Sunday

Weekly

Monday

Tuesday

Wednesday

Thursday

Friday

Saturday

Sunday

Weekly

Monday

Tuesday

Wednesday

Thursday

Friday

Saturday

Sunday

Weekly

Monday

Tuesday

Wednesday

Thursday

Friday

Saturday

Sunday

Weekly

Monday

Tuesday

Wednesday

Thursday

Friday

Saturday

Sunday

Reflection

Reflect on your month, what went well, and what didn't. Use this space to download the good, the bad and the ugly. Transfer any ideas to the master task lists or add them to your journalling prompts for more clarity, or if you want to dig a bit deeper.

Notes / Ideas

Live as if you were to die tomorrow. Learn as if you were to live forever.

Mahatma Gandhi

Monthly Goals

Wealth & Abundance:	Fame & Reputation:	Relationships & Love
Focuses on prosperity, financial well being, and material abundance.	Represents your public image, recognition, and how others see you.	Governs romantic and personal relationships.
Health:	**Knowledge & Wisdom:**	**Career & Life Path:**
Focusing on your health and balance, as well as your physical, emotional, and mental health in all areas of life.	This area focuses on learning, personal development, and self-cultivation.	This area relates to your career, life's journey, and purpose.
Helpful People & Travel:	**Children & Creativity:**	**Family & Ancestors:**
This sector governs the presence of mentors, helpful people, and travel opportunities.	Connected to creativity, joy, and future projects, including children.	Strengthening and bringing harmony in relationships with family.

Align & Begin

Journal all or some of these questions

How do I feel? What do I want to achieve? What do I want to clear?

Journal Prompts

For more clarity, use the space below to record anything that came up while journaling. Bullet below, and use the memory, question, thought, or emotion as a journal prompt when you feel ready.

-
-
-
-
-
-
-
-
-
-
-
-
-
-
-
-
-
-
-
-
-
-
-
-

Month to View

1.
2.
3.
4.
5.
6.
7.
8.
9.
10.
11.
12.
13.
14.
15.
16.
17.
18.
19.
20.
21.
22.
23.
24.
25.
26.
27.
28.
29.
30.
31.

Tasks

Weekly

Monday

Tuesday

Wednesday

Thursday

Friday

Saturday

Sunday

Weekly

Monday

Tuesday

Wednesday

Thursday

Friday

Saturday

Sunday

Weekly

Monday

Tuesday

Wednesday

Thursday

Friday

Saturday

Sunday

Weekly

Monday

Tuesday

Wednesday

Thursday

Friday

Saturday

Sunday

Weekly

Monday

Tuesday

Wednesday

Thursday

Friday

Saturday

Sunday

Reflection

Reflect on your month, what went well, and what didn't. Use this space to download the good, the bad and the ugly. Transfer any ideas to the master task lists or add them to your journalling prompts for more clarity, or if you want to dig a bit deeper.

Notes / Ideas

Human knowledge consists not only of libraries of parchment and ink - it is also comprised of the volumes of knowledge that are written on the human heart, chiselled on the human soul, and engraved on the human psyche.

Michael Jackson

Monthly Goals

Wealth & Abundance: Focuses on prosperity, financial well being, and material abundance.	**Fame & Reputation:** Represents your public image, recognition, and how others see you.	**Relationships & Love** Governs romantic and personal relationships.
Health: Focusing on your health and balance, as well as your physical, emotional, and mental health in all areas of life.	**Knowledge & Wisdom:** This area focuses on learning, personal development, and self-cultivation.	**Career & Life Path:** This area relates to your career, life's journey, and purpose.
Helpful People & Travel: This sector governs the presence of mentors, helpful people, and travel opportunities.	**Children & Creativity:** Connected to creativity, joy, and future projects, including children.	**Family & Ancestors:** Strengthening and bringing harmony in relationships with family.

Align & Begin

Journal all or some of these questions

How do I feel? What do I want to achieve? What do I want to clear?

Journal Prompts

For more clarity, use the space below to record anything that came up while journaling. Bullet below, and use the memory, question, thought, or emotion as a journal prompt when you feel ready.

-
-
-
-
-
-
-
-
-
-
-
-
-
-
-
-
-
-
-
-
-
-
-
-

Month to View

1.
2.
3.
4.
5.
6.
7.
8.
9.
10.
11.
12.
13.
14.
15.
16.
17.
18.
19.
20.
21.
22.
23.
24.
25.
26.
27.
28.
29.
30.
31.

Tasks

Weekly

Monday

Tuesday

Wednesday

Thursday

Friday

Saturday

Sunday

Weekly

Monday

Tuesday

Wednesday

Thursday

Friday

Saturday

Sunday

Weekly

Monday

Tuesday

Wednesday

Thursday

Friday

Saturday

Sunday

Weekly

Monday

Tuesday

Wednesday

Thursday

Friday

Saturday

Sunday

Weekly

Monday

Tuesday

Wednesday

Thursday

Friday

Saturday

Sunday

Reflection

Reflect on your month, what went well, and what didn't. Use this space to download the good, the bad and the ugly. Transfer any ideas to the master task lists or add them to your journalling prompts for more clarity, or if you want to dig a bit deeper.

Notes / Ideas

113

"

Safety is not the absence of threat; it is the presence of connection.

Gabor Mate

Monthly Goals

Wealth & Abundance:
Focuses on prosperity, financial well being, and material abundance.

Fame & Reputation:
Represents your public image, recognition, and how others see you.

Relationships & Love
Governs romantic and personal relationships.

Health:
Focusing on your health and balance, as well as your physical, emotional, and mental health in all areas of life.

Knowledge & Wisdom:
This area focuses on learning, personal development, and self-cultivation.

Career & Life Path:
This area relates to your career, life's journey, and purpose.

Helpful People & Travel:
This sector governs the presence of mentors, helpful people, and travel opportunities.

Children & Creativity:
Connected to creativity, joy, and future projects, including children.

Family & Ancestors:
Strengthening and bringing harmony in relationships with family.

Align & Begin

Journal all or some of these questions
How do I feel? What do I want to achieve? What do I want to clear?

Journal Prompts

For more clarity, use the space below to record anything that came up while journaling. Bullet below, and use the memory, question, thought, or emotion as a journal prompt when you feel ready.

-
-
-
-
-
-
-
-
-
-
-
-
-
-
-
-
-
-
-
-
-
-
-
-

Month to View

1.
2.
3.
4.
5.
6.
7.
8.
9.
10.
11.
12.
13.
14.
15.
16.
17.
18.
19.
20.
21.
22.
23.
24.
25.
26.
27.
28.
29.
30.
31.

Tasks

Weekly

Monday

Tuesday

Wednesday

Thursday

Friday

Saturday

Sunday

Weekly

Monday

Tuesday

Wednesday

Thursday

Friday

Saturday

Sunday

Weekly

Monday

Tuesday

Wednesday

Thursday

Friday

Saturday

Sunday

Weekly

Monday

Tuesday

Wednesday

Thursday

Friday

Saturday

Sunday

Weekly

Monday

Tuesday

Wednesday

Thursday

Friday

Saturday

Sunday

Reflection

Reflect on your month, what went well, and what didn't. Use this space to download the good, the bad and the ugly. Transfer any ideas to the master task lists or add them to your journalling prompts for more clarity, or if you want to dig a bit deeper.

Notes / Ideas

141

> Watch your thoughts; they become words. Watch your words; they become actions. Watch your actions; they become habits. Watch your habits; they become character. Watch your character; it becomes your destiny.
> Lao-Tze

Monthly Goals

Wealth & Abundance: Focuses on prosperity, financial well being, and material abundance.	**Fame & Reputation:** Represents your public image, recognition, and how others see you.	**Relationships & Love** Governs romantic and personal relationships.
Health: Focusing on your health and balance, as well as your physical, emotional, and mental health in all areas of life.	**Knowledge & Wisdom:** This area focuses on learning, personal development, and self-cultivation.	**Career & Life Path:** This area relates to your career, life's journey, and purpose.
Helpful People & Travel: This sector governs the presence of mentors, helpful people, and travel opportunities.	**Children & Creativity:** Connected to creativity, joy, and future projects, including children.	**Family & Ancestors:** Strengthening and bringing harmony in relationships with family.

Align & Begin

Journal all or some of these questions

How do I feel? What do I want to achieve? What do I want to clear?

Journal Prompts

For more clarity, use the space below to record anything that came up while journaling. Bullet below, and use the memory, question, thought, or emotion as a journal prompt when you feel ready.

Month to View

1.
2.
3.
4.
5.
6.
7.
8.
9.
10.
11.
12.
13.
14.
15.
16.
17.
18.
19.
20.
21.
22.
23.
24.
25.
26.
27.
28.
29.
30.
31.

Tasks

Weekly

Monday

Tuesday

Wednesday

Thursday

Friday

Saturday

Sunday

Weekly

Monday

Tuesday

Wednesday

Thursday

Friday

Saturday

Sunday

Weekly

Monday

Tuesday

Wednesday

Thursday

Friday

Saturday

Sunday

Weekly

Monday

Tuesday

Wednesday

| Thursday |

| Friday |

| Saturday |

| Sunday |

Weekly

Monday

Tuesday

Wednesday

Thursday

Friday

Saturday

Sunday

Reflection

Reflect on your month, what went well, and what didn't. Use this space to download the good, the bad and the ugly. Transfer any ideas to the master task lists or add them to your journalling prompts for more clarity, or if you want to dig a bit deeper.

Notes / Ideas

> "In life, be a warrior, not a worrier. Conquer your doubts, face your fears, and pursue your dreams.
> Unknown

Monthly Goals

Wealth & Abundance: Focuses on prosperity, financial well being, and material abundance.	**Fame & Reputation:** Represents your public image, recognition, and how others see you.	**Relationships & Love** Governs romantic and personal relationships.
Health: Focusing on your health and balance, as well as your physical, emotional, and mental health in all areas of life.	**Knowledge & Wisdom:** This area focuses on learning, personal development, and self-cultivation.	**Career & Life Path:** This area relates to your career, life's journey, and purpose.
Helpful People & Travel: This sector governs the presence of mentors, helpful people, and travel opportunities.	**Children & Creativity:** Connected to creativity, joy, and future projects, including children.	**Family & Ancestors:** Strengthening and bringing harmony in relationships with family.

Align & Begin

Journal all or some of these questions

How do I feel? What do I want to achieve? What do I want to clear?

Journal Prompts

For more clarity, use the space below to record anything that came up while journaling. Bullet below, and use the memory, question, thought, or emotion as a journal prompt when you feel ready.

-
-
-
-
-
-
-
-
-
-
-
-
-
-
-
-
-
-
-
-
-
-
-
-

Month to View

1.
2.
3.
4.
5.
6.
7.
8.
9.
10.
11.
12.
13.
14.
15.
16.
17.
18.
19.
20.
21.
22.
23.
24.
25.
26.
27.
28.
29.
30.
31.

Tasks

Weekly

Monday

Tuesday

Wednesday

Thursday

Friday

Saturday

Sunday

Weekly

Monday

Tuesday

Wednesday

Thursday

Friday

Saturday

Sunday

Weekly

Monday

Tuesday

Wednesday

Thursday

Friday

Saturday	Sunday

Weekly

Monday

Tuesday

Wednesday

Thursday

Friday

Saturday

Sunday

Weekly

Monday

Tuesday

Wednesday

Thursday

Friday

Saturday

Sunday

Reflection

Reflect on your month, what went well, and what didn't. Use this space to download the good, the bad and the ugly. Transfer any ideas to the master task lists or add them to your journalling prompts for more clarity, or if you want to dig a bit deeper.

Notes / Ideas

"

The journey is learning that pain, like love, is simply something to surrender to. It's a holy space we can enter with people only if we promise not to tidy up.

Glennon Doyle

Monthly Goals

Wealth & Abundance: Focuses on prosperity, financial well being, and material abundance.	**Fame & Reputation:** Represents your public image, recognition, and how others see you.	**Relationships & Love** Governs romantic and personal relationships.
Health: Focusing on your health and balance, as well as your physical, emotional, and mental health in all areas of life.	**Knowledge & Wisdom:** This area focuses on learning, personal development, and self-cultivation.	**Career & Life Path:** This area relates to your career, life's journey, and purpose.
Helpful People & Travel: This sector governs the presence of mentors, helpful people, and travel opportunities.	**Children & Creativity:** Connected to creativity, joy, and future projects, including children.	**Family & Ancestors:** Strengthening and bringing harmony in relationships with family.

Align & Begin

Journal all or some of these questions

How do I feel? What do I want to achieve? What do I want to clear?

Journal Prompts

For more clarity, use the space below to record anything that came up while journaling. Bullet below, and use the memory, question, thought, or emotion as a journal prompt when you feel ready.

-
-
-
-
-
-
-
-
-
-
-
-
-
-
-
-
-
-
-
-
-
-
-
-

Month to View

1.
2.
3.
4.
5.
6.
7.
8.
9.
10.
11.
12.
13.
14.
15.
16.
17.
18.
19.
20.
21.
22.
23.
24.
25.
26.
27.
28.
29.
30.
31.

Tasks

Weekly

Monday

Tuesday

Wednesday

Thursday

Friday

Saturday

Sunday

Weekly

Monday

Tuesday

Wednesday

Thursday

Friday

Saturday

Sunday

Weekly

Monday

Tuesday

Wednesday

Thursday

Friday

Saturday

Sunday

Weekly

Monday

Tuesday

Wednesday

Thursday

Friday

Saturday	Sunday

Weekly

Monday

Tuesday

Wednesday

Thursday

Friday

Saturday

Sunday

Reflection

Reflect on your month, what went well, and what didn't. Use this space to download the good, the bad and the ugly. Transfer any ideas to the master task lists or add them to your journalling prompts for more clarity, or if you want to dig a bit deeper.

Notes / Ideas

217

> Until you make the unconscious conscious, it will direct your life and you will call it fate.
> Carl Jung

Monthly Goals

Wealth & Abundance: Focuses on prosperity, financial well being, and material abundance.	**Fame & Reputation:** Represents your public image, recognition, and how others see you.	**Relationships & Love** Governs romantic and personal relationships.
Health: Focusing on your health and balance, as well as your physical, emotional, and mental health in all areas of life.	**Knowledge & Wisdom:** This area focuses on learning, personal development, and self-cultivation.	**Career & Life Path:** This area relates to your career, life's journey, and purpose.
Helpful People & Travel: This sector governs the presence of mentors, helpful people, and travel opportunities.	**Children & Creativity:** Connected to creativity, joy, and future projects, including children.	**Family & Ancestors:** Strengthening and bringing harmony in relationships with family.

Align & Begin

Journal all or some of these questions
How do I feel? What do I want to achieve? What do I want to clear?

Journal Prompts

For more clarity, use the space below to record anything that came up while journaling. Bullet below, and use the memory, question, thought, or emotion as a journal prompt when you feel ready.

Month to View

1
2
3
4
5
6
7
8
9
10
11
12
13
14
15
16
17
18
19
20
21
22
23
24
25
26
27
28
29
30
31

Tasks

Weekly

Monday

Tuesday

Wednesday

Thursday

Friday

Saturday

Sunday

Weekly

Monday

Tuesday

Wednesday

Thursday

Friday

Saturday

Sunday

Weekly

Monday

Tuesday

Wednesday

Thursday

Friday

Saturday

Sunday

Weekly

Monday

Tuesday

Wednesday

Thursday

Friday

Saturday

Sunday

Weekly

Monday

Tuesday

Wednesday

Thursday

Friday

Saturday

Sunday

Reflection

Reflect on your month, what went well, and what didn't. Use this space to download the good, the bad and the ugly. Transfer any ideas to the master task lists or add them to your journalling prompts for more clarity, or if you want to dig a bit deeper.

Notes / Ideas

243

"The body remembers, the bones remember, the joints remember, even the little finger remembers. Memory is lodged in pictures and feelings in the cells themselves. Like a sponge filled with water, anywhere the flesh is pressed, wrung, even touched lightly, a memory may flow out in a stream.

Clarissa Pinkola Estes

Monthly Goals

Wealth & Abundance: Focuses on prosperity, financial well being, and material abundance.	**Fame & Reputation:** Represents your public image, recognition, and how others see you.	**Relationships & Love** Governs romantic and personal relationships.
Health: Focusing on your health and balance, as well as your physical, emotional, and mental health in all areas of life.	**Knowledge & Wisdom:** This area focuses on learning, personal development, and self-cultivation.	**Career & Life Path:** This area relates to your career, life's journey, and purpose.
Helpful People & Travel: This sector governs the presence of mentors, helpful people, and travel opportunities.	**Children & Creativity:** Connected to creativity, joy, and future projects, including children.	**Family & Ancestors:** Strengthening and bringing harmony in relationships with family.

Align & Begin

Journal all or some of these questions

How do I feel? What do I want to achieve? What do I want to clear?

Journal Prompts

For more clarity, use the space below to record anything that came up while journaling. Bullet below, and use the memory, question, thought, or emotion as a journal prompt when you feel ready.

-
-
-
-
-
-
-
-
-
-
-
-
-
-
-
-
-
-
-
-
-
-
-
-

Month to View

1.
2.
3.
4.
5.
6.
7.
8.
9.
10.
11.
12.
13.
14.
15.
16.
17.
18.
19.
20.
21.
22.
23.
24.
25.
26.
27.
28.
29.
30.
31.

Tasks

Weekly

Monday

Tuesday

Wednesday

Thursday

Friday

Saturday

Sunday

Weekly

Monday

Tuesday

Wednesday

Thursday

Friday

Saturday

Sunday

Weekly

Monday

Tuesday

Wednesday

Thursday

Friday

Saturday

Sunday

Weekly

Monday

Tuesday

Wednesday

Thursday

Friday

Saturday

Sunday

Weekly

Monday

Tuesday

Wednesday

Thursday

Friday

Saturday	Sunday

Reflection

Reflect on your month, what went well, and what didn't. Use this space to download the good, the bad and the ugly. Transfer any ideas to the master task lists or add them to your journalling prompts for more clarity, or if you want to dig a bit deeper.

Notes / Ideas

It is time to search out your uniqueness, applaud and acknowledge yourself, and let your own light shine.

Debbie Ford

Monthly Goals

Wealth & Abundance: Focuses on prosperity, financial well being, and material abundance.	**Fame & Reputation:** Represents your public image, recognition, and how others see you.	**Relationships & Love** Governs romantic and personal relationships.
Health: Focusing on your health and balance, as well as your physical, emotional, and mental health in all areas of life.	**Knowledge & Wisdom:** This area focuses on learning, personal development, and self-cultivation.	**Career & Life Path:** This area relates to your career, life's journey, and purpose.
Helpful People & Travel: This sector governs the presence of mentors, helpful people, and travel opportunities.	**Children & Creativity:** Connected to creativity, joy, and future projects, including children.	**Family & Ancestors:** Strengthening and bringing harmony in relationships with family.

Align & Begin

Journal all or some of these questions
How do I feel? What do I want to achieve? What do I want to clear?

Journal Prompts

For more clarity, use the space below to record anything that came up while journaling. Bullet below, and use the memory, question, thought, or emotion as a journal prompt when you feel ready.

-
-
-
-
-
-
-
-
-
-
-
-
-
-
-
-
-
-
-
-
-
-
-
-

Month to View

1
2
3
4
5
6
7
8
9
10
11
12
13
14
15
16
17
18
19
20
21
22
23
24
25
26
27
28
29
30
31

Tasks

Weekly

Monday

Tuesday

Wednesday

Thursday

Friday

Saturday

Sunday

Weekly

Monday

Tuesday

Wednesday

Thursday

Friday

Saturday

Sunday

Weekly

Monday

Tuesday

Wednesday

Thursday

Friday

Saturday

Sunday

Weekly

Monday

Tuesday

Wednesday

Thursday

Friday

Saturday

Sunday

Weekly

Monday

Tuesday

Wednesday

Thursday

Friday

Saturday

Sunday

Reflection

Reflect on your month, what went well, and what didn't. Use this space to download the good, the bad and the ugly. Transfer any ideas to the master task lists or add them to your journalling prompts for more clarity, or if you want to dig a bit deeper.

Notes / Ideas

> You aren't a machine with broken parts. You are an animal whose needs are not being met. You need to have a community. You need to have meaningful values, not the junk values you've been pumped full of all your life, telling you happiness comes through money and buying objects. You need to have meaningful work. You need the natural world. You need to feel you are respected. You need a secure future. You need connections to all these things. You need to release any shame you might feel for having been mistreated.
>
> Johann Hari, Lost Connections

Monthly Goals

Wealth & Abundance:
Focuses on prosperity, financial well being, and material abundance.

Fame & Reputation:
Represents your public image, recognition, and how others see you.

Relationships & Love
Governs romantic and personal relationships.

Health:
Focusing on your health and balance, as well as your physical, emotional, and mental health in all areas of life.

Knowledge & Wisdom:
This area focuses on learning, personal development, and self-cultivation.

Career & Life Path:
This area relates to your career, life's journey, and purpose.

Helpful People & Travel:
This sector governs the presence of mentors, helpful people, and travel opportunities.

Children & Creativity:
Connected to creativity, joy, and future projects, including children.

Family & Ancestors:
Strengthening and bringing harmony in relationships with family.

Align & Begin

Journal all or some of these questions
How do I feel? What do I want to achieve? What do I want to clear?

Journal Prompts

For more clarity, use the space below to record anything that came up while journaling. Bullet below, and use the memory, question, thought, or emotion as a journal prompt when you feel ready.

-
-
-
-
-
-
-
-
-
-
-
-
-
-
-
-
-
-
-
-
-
-
-
-

Month to View

1.
2.
3.
4.
5.
6.
7.
8.
9.
10.
11.
12.
13.
14.
15.
16.
17.
18.
19.
20.
21.
22.
23.
24.
25.
26.
27.
28.
29.
30.
31.

Tasks

Weekly

Monday

Tuesday

Wednesday

Thursday

Friday

Saturday

Sunday

Weekly

Monday

Tuesday

Wednesday

Thursday

Friday

Saturday

Sunday

Weekly

Monday

Tuesday

Wednesday

Thursday

Friday

Saturday

Sunday

Weekly

Monday

Tuesday

Wednesday

Thursday

Friday

Saturday

Sunday

Weekly

Monday

Tuesday

Wednesday

Thursday

Friday

Saturday

Sunday

Reflection

Reflect on your month, what went well, and what didn't. Use this space to download the good, the bad and the ugly. Transfer any ideas to the master task lists or add them to your journalling prompts for more clarity, or if you want to dig a bit deeper.

Notes / Ideas

> You have been assigned this Mountain so that you can show others it can be moved.
>
> Mel Robbins

Monthly Goals

Wealth & Abundance: Focuses on prosperity, financial well being, and material abundance.	**Fame & Reputation:** Represents your public image, recognition, and how others see you.	**Relationships & Love** Governs romantic and personal relationships.
Health: Focusing on your health and balance, as well as your physical, emotional, and mental health in all areas of life.	**Knowledge & Wisdom:** This area focuses on learning, personal development, and self-cultivation.	**Career & Life Path:** This area relates to your career, life's journey, and purpose.
Helpful People & Travel: This sector governs the presence of mentors, helpful people, and travel opportunities.	**Children & Creativity:** Connected to creativity, joy, and future projects, including children.	**Family & Ancestors:** Strengthening and bringing harmony in relationships with family.

Align & Begin

Journal all or some of these questions

How do I feel? What do I want to achieve? What do I want to clear?

Journal Prompts

For more clarity, use the space below to record anything that came up while journaling. Bullet below, and use the memory, question, thought, or emotion as a journal prompt when you feel ready.

-
-
-
-
-
-
-
-
-
-
-
-
-
-
-
-
-
-
-
-
-
-
-
-

Month to View

1.
2.
3.
4.
5.
6.
7.
8.
9.
10.
11.
12.
13.
14.
15.
16.
17.
18.
19.
20.
21.
22.
23.
24.
25.
26.
27.
28.
29.
30.
31.

Tasks

Weekly

Monday

Tuesday

Wednesday

Thursday

Friday

Saturday

Sunday

Weekly

Monday

Tuesday

Wednesday

Thursday

Friday

Saturday

Sunday

Weekly

Monday

Tuesday

Wednesday

Thursday

Friday

Saturday

Sunday

Weekly

Monday

Tuesday

Wednesday

Thursday

Friday

Saturday

Sunday

Weekly

Monday

Tuesday

Wednesday

Thursday

Friday

Saturday

Sunday

Reflection

Reflect on your month, what went well, and what didn't. Use this space to download the good, the bad and the ugly. Transfer any ideas to the master task lists or add them to your journalling prompts for more clarity, or if you want to dig a bit deeper.

Notes / Ideas

Quote References

1. https://www.goodreads.com/quotes/512-there-is-no-greater-agony-than-bearingan-untold-story
2. https://www.brainyquote.com/quotes/confucius_104563
3. https://www.amazon.co.uk/Finding-Lily-Elizabeth-Goddard/dp/0995537518/ref=cm_cr_arp_d_product_top?ie=UTF8
4. https://www.brainyquote.com/quotes/mahatma_gandhi_133995
5. https://www.goodreads.com/quotes/208753-human-knowledge-consists-notonly-of-libraries-of-parchment-and
6. https://borettiinc.com/safety-is-not-the-absence-of-threat-it-is-the-presence-ofconnection/
7. https://quoteinvestigator.com/2013/01/10/watch-your-thoughts/
8. https://sandjest.com/blogs/quotes/life-lesson-quotes
9. https://www.goodreads.com/quotes/7781134-the-journey-is-learning-that-painlike-love-is-simply
10. https://www.goodreads.com/quotes/44379-until-you-make-the-unconsciousconscious-it-will-direct-your
11. https://www.goodreads.com/quotes/8954946-the-body-is-a-multilingual-being-itspeaks-through-its
12. https://www.azquotes.com/quote/882674
13. 1https://www.goodreads.com/quotes/9265083-you-aren-t-a-machine-with-brokenparts-you-are-an
14. https://quotefancy.com/quote/2672380/Mel-Robbins-You-have-been-assignedthis-mountain-so-that-you-can-show-others-it-can-be

www.ingramcontent.com/pod-product-compliance
Lightning Source LLC
Chambersburg PA
CBHW051329110526
44590CB00032B/4464